Big Dips

james bradford

GIBBS SMITH
TO ENRICH AND INSPIRE HUMANKIND

Contents

Introduction

As a chef, I get asked all the time, "Do you ever get tired of cooking?" and the answer is still no! The only thing I enjoy more than cooking is sharing the food I create with other people. I jump at the chance to cook at any friend or family event, and even when I am planning on staying out of the kitchen, I usually end up with an apron on, standing over the stove.

Because I love cooking, I am the kind of guy that can't be happy to just make dinner. I have to set out something when people arrive, usually a canapé that I can quickly assemble while talking to my guests. One thing I have learned over all of the years that I have been cooking, whether for work or at home, is that people love to snack before they eat! Having a bowl of hummus and some veggies can buy you an extra thirty minutes to finish up that rib roast or boil the potatoes just a little bit longer without anyone asking where the food is.

I don't let anything go to waste either. Dips can have a life beyond the cracker or crostini. Having a bit of leftover pesto in the fridge can give you an extra layer of flavor that you didn't realize that salad dressing needed, and having a bit of cheese dip on hand can turn a cream sauce into a smoked-Gouda masterpiece that even *you* didn't see coming!

But what are dips really made for? Parties! The recipes in this book are all quick and easy to make. Nearly every one of them can be prepared without the stove or the oven. All you need is a blender or food processor and your ingredients, and you're ready to get cooking! (Yes, it still counts as cooking in my book.) Make a last-minute batch of sweet and piquant Pineapple and Cilantro Salsa (page 35) for that Cinco de Mayo party you almost forgot about, or whip up a simple yet sophisticated Truffle Dip (page 117) for your next book club meeting. Double the recipes to (hopefully) have leftovers for perking up your dinner or for after-school or pre-dinner snacks the next day.

Each of these recipes is tasty, crowd-pleasing, and just plain fun to make. I encourage you to be adventurous with these dips. Get brave and bold in your kitchen; change up the recipes a bit if you have an ingredient in mind that can make a dip even better. I usually treat recipes more like suggestions, and I think you'd have a blast if you did too. Work through a few of the dips in each chapter and get a feel for what making dips, pesto, hummus, and salsa is all about, then try your hand at adding a bit of your own flavor. It may take a few adjustments to get it just right, but that can be half the fun. Plus, there is nothing like taking a recipe and turning it into a dish that you get to own and brag about! But before you start dipping, you'll need some dippers.

In the next few pages, you'll find recipes for Basic Crostini, Ciabatta Toast, Crispy Pita Wedges, and Tortilla Chips. Don't limit yourself to these classic options, though; try zucchini sticks, sweet peppers, potato wedges, or any other finger food you enjoy. Now, let's get dipping!

Big Dippers

CIABATTA TOAST

Makes 30 to 40 slices

1 loaf ciabatta bread, cut into
  $1/4$-inch-thick slices about 2 inches
  long

1 stick unsalted butter

Salt

Preheat the oven to 400°F. Grease a baking sheet and set aside.

Heat a large nonstick skillet over medium heat. Working in batches, melt enough butter to cover the bottom of the pan and dip both sides of each piece of ciabatta in the melted butter. Arrange the buttered pieces on the baking sheet and bake for 10 to 12 minutes, until browned and crispy to the center. Allow to cool at room temperature. Repeat until all of the ciabatta has been toasted.

BASIC CROSTINI

Makes about 60 slices

1 (8- to 10-ounce) baguette,* cut into
    1/4-inch-thick slices

3/4 cup olive oil

Salt

1 cup grated Parmesan

1/4 cup minced fresh parsley

Preheat the oven to 425°F. Grease a baking sheet. Arrange the baguette slices on the sheet in a single layer as close together as possible. Set aside any slices that do not fit. Drizzle the bread lightly with olive oil, then sprinkle with salt. Sprinkle the slices with the Parmesan and parsley. Bake for 10 to 12 minutes, or until the edges are lightly browned and the bread is a bit crispy. Allow to cool at room temperature. Repeat until all of the baguette slices have been baked.

Many supermarkets offer a variety of artisanal loaves that would work well for this recipe. The trick is to select bread with a dense interior that will crisp up well and allow for scooping without breaking. Another thing to keep in mind when making crostini is that they should fit in your mouth in one or two bites.

TORTILLA CHIPS

Makes 72 chips

12 corn tortillas, each cut into 6 triangles

Vegetable or canola oil, for frying

Kosher salt

Fill a cast-iron Dutch oven or heavy-bottomed saucepot with roughly 1 inch of oil. Place over medium heat and bring the oil up to 350°F, measuring with a candy or deep-fryer thermometer. Place about a quarter of the triangles in the hot oil; stir gently to ensure they cook evenly on all sides. Continue to fry until the edges begin to brown and the tortillas are no longer pliable. Using a slotted spoon or wire strainer, remove the chips from the oil and drain well. While still warm, place the chips into a large bowl and toss with a large pinch of kosher salt. Continue working in batches until all of the tortillas have been fried and tossed in salt.

VARIATION: For baked tortilla chips, place the cut tortillas in a single layer on a parchment-lined baking sheet. Bake at 350°F for 5 to 6 minutes. Turn the tortillas over and continue to bake until lightly browned and firm in the center, about 5 minutes. When the chips are crispy, remove them from the oven. Toss with kosher salt while still warm.

CRISPY PITA WEDGES

Makes 40 wedges

5 (6-inch) pitas, each cut into 8 wedges

$1/4$ cup olive oil

Salt

Preheat the oven to 400°F. Grease a baking sheet. Arrange the pita wedges on the baking sheet as close together as possible, then drizzle lightly with olive oil and sprinkle with salt. Bake for 10 to 12 minutes, until the pita is just browned and slightly crisp. Depending on the size of your baking sheet, you may need to bake the wedges in multiple batches.

CHEESE

All of these cheese dips are great served cold, but to make a dip easier to spread, put it into a baking dish and warm it up at 350°F for 10 minutes. The dips pair well with something crispy, like crostini, but even a piece of sourdough bread cut into bite-size pieces would do the trick. A bit of crunch from the dipper provides great textural contrast, but what I really look for in a cheese dip is a distinctive flavor—the sweet kick of figs or the salty bite of capers can really set it apart.

Impress your friends with fresh, crisp vegetables served with a goat cheese dip loaded with herbs out of your own garden, or show up to a party with a bowl of Jalapeño Cheddar Dip (page 19) and a bagful of just-baked Tortilla Chips (page 8). The one that always gets eaten quickly around my house is the Sweet and Salty Ham and Fig Dip (page 27). My kids were a bit leery at first, but now I barely get any for myself!

Pear and Walnut Dip

Makes about 2 cups

1 cup ricotta cheese

$1/2$ cup grated provolone cheese

$1/2$ cup diced pears

$1/2$ cup chopped walnuts

2 tablespoons honey

$1/4$ teaspoon salt

In a large bowl, combine the ricotta, provolone, and pears; mix with a spoon until well blended. In a small bowl, combine the walnuts, honey, and salt; stir until the walnuts are well coated. Transfer the cheese mix to a serving bowl and top with the honeyed walnuts.

VARIATION: Substitute a portion of the walnuts for pecans, cashews, chestnuts, or any other nuts you may have. Using a batch of mixed nuts left over from the holidays is a fantastic choice.

Crab Ball

Makes about 2 cups

1 (8-ounce) package cream cheese, at room temperature

1 tablespoon minced fresh chives

1/2 small red onion, minced

1/2 teaspoon Old Bay seasoning

1 teaspoon freshly squeezed lemon juice

1 tablespoon capers

1 (6-ounce) can crabmeat

1/2 cup sliced almonds (optional)

In a large bowl, combine the cream cheese, chives, red onion, Old Bay seasoning, lemon juice, and capers; mix with a spoon until well blended. Gently fold the crabmeat into the cream cheese mixture, being careful not to break up the crab too much. Split the mixture into two equal portions. Using your hands, shape each portion into a rough sphere. (They don't have to be perfect.) Place the sliced almonds in a shallow dish and roll each crab ball in them to coat. Place the crab balls on a plate and chill in the fridge for 2 hours, or overnight, before serving.

VARIATION: If you are not fond of almonds, you can roll your crab ball in minced fresh parsley, minced fresh chives, or even toasted panko breadcrumbs.

Buffalo Blue Cheese Chicken Dip

Makes about 3 cups

1 (8-ounce) package cream cheese, at room temperature

$^1/_4$ cup Frank's hot sauce

$^1/_2$ cup blue cheese crumbles, divided

$^1/_2$ cup grated cheddar cheese

$^1/_2$ pound shredded cooked chicken, or 1 (12.5-ounce can) chicken breast

In a large bowl, combine the cream cheese, hot sauce, and $^1/_4$ cup of the blue cheese; mix with a spoon until well blended. Fold in the cheddar cheese and chicken. Top with the remaining blue cheese.

VARIATION: If you are a fan of the celery and carrots that often come with buffalo wings, fold in $^1/_4$ cup minced celery and $^1/_4$ cup minced carrots with the chicken.

Gruyère and Olive Spread

Makes about 2 cups

1 clove garlic, minced

1 (8-ounce) package cream cheese, at room temperature

1 cup ricotta cheese

$1/2$ teaspoon black pepper

1 cup large green olives, chopped

1 cup grated Gruyère cheese

Sliced green olives, for garnish

In a large bowl, combine the garlic, cream cheese, ricotta, and pepper; mix with a spoon until well blended. Fold in the olives and Gruyère cheese. Transfer to a serving dish and garnish with sliced olives.

VARIATION: The Gruyère can be substituted with any cheese that is bold and not too salty, like Munster or Gouda. For another layer of flavor, add 1 tablespoon minced fresh rosemary.

Jalapeño Cheddar Dip

Makes about 2 cups

1 (8-ounce) package cream cheese, at room temperature

1/2 cup mayonnaise

1 (4-ounce) can diced green chiles

Juice of 1 lemon

4 jalapeños, seeded and minced

1/2 cup grated Parmesan cheese

1 cup grated cheddar cheese

In a large bowl, combine the cream cheese, mayonnaise, green chiles, lemon juice, and jalapeños; mix with a spoon until well blended. Fold in the cheddar and Parmesan cheese.

VARIATION: For Jalapeño Popper Dip, fold in 1/2 cup chopped crispy-cooked bacon with the cheese.

Smoked Salmon Dip

Makes about 2 cups

1 (8-ounce) package cream cheese, at
    room temperature

1/2 teaspoon Worcestershire sauce

1 teaspoon fresh dill

2 tablespoons minced fresh chives

1 tablespoon capers

8 ounces smoked salmon

In a large bowl, combine the cream cheese, Worcestershire, dill, chives, and capers; mix with a spoon until well blended. Gently break the smoked salmon into small pieces and fold into the cheese mix, being careful not to break up the fish too much.

VARIATIONS: For Smoked Salmon Pâté, blend the ingredients in a food processor until smooth. For Smoked Salmon Mousse, whip 1 cup heavy cream to soft peaks and fold in the Smoked Salmon Pâté. Refrigerate for 2 hours before serving to set.

Cranberry Pecan Dip

Makes about 2 cups

1 (8-ounce) package cream cheese, at
   room temperature

Zest and juice of 1 orange

1 tablespoon grated fresh ginger

1 tablespoon brown sugar

$^1/_2$ cup dried cranberries, chopped

$^1/_2$ cup toasted pecans, chopped

In a large bowl, combine the cream cheese, orange zest and juice, ginger, and brown sugar; mix with a spoon until well blended. Fold in the cranberries and pecans.

VARIATION: If you want a slightly sweeter dip with some holiday spice to it, add 1 tablespoon honey, $^1/_2$ teaspoon ground cinnamon, $^1/_4$ teaspoon ground allspice, $^1/_4$ teaspoon ground ginger, and a pinch of ground cloves before mixing.

Pretzels and Beer Cheese

Makes about 3 cups

1 (8-ounce) package cream cheese, at room temperature

2 cloves garlic, minced

1 teaspoon fresh dill

1 teaspoon minced fresh parsley

1 teaspoon freshly squeezed lemon juice

$1/2$ teaspoon salt

1 teaspoon black pepper

$1/3$ cup dark beer, such as Guinness, or Pilsner, such as Corona

1 cup grated cheddar cheese

1 cup grated Swiss cheese

$1/2$ cup crushed pretzels

In a large bowl, combine the cream cheese, garlic, dill, parsley, lemon juice, salt, pepper, and beer; mix with a wire whisk until well blended. Fold in the cheddar and Swiss cheeses. Transfer to a serving bowl and top with crushed pretzels.

VARIATION: Instead of topping with crushed pretzels, serve with whole pretzels for dipping.

Sweet and Salty Ham and Fig Dip

Makes about 2 cups

½ cup mayonnaise

2 cloves garlic, minced

¼ cup dried Mission figs, sliced

½ cup diced Black Forest ham

2 tablespoons minced fresh rosemary

½ teaspoon black pepper

1 cup grated Swiss cheese

In a large bowl, combine the mayonnaise, garlic, figs, ham, rosemary, and pepper; mix with a wire whisk until well blended. Fold in the Swiss cheese.

VARIATION: Substitute a portion of the ham for another cured pork product such as prosciutto cotto, crispy pancetta, or Genoa salami.

Herbed Goat Cheese

Makes about 2 cups

$^3/_4$ cup soft goat cheese

$^1/_2$ cup ricotta cheese

$^1/_4$ cup finely grated mozzarella cheese

1 tablespoon chopped fresh thyme

1 tablespoon chopped fresh sage

1 teaspoon freshly squeezed lemon juice

Freshly cracked black pepper

In a large bowl, combine the goat cheese, ricotta cheese, mozzarella cheese, thyme, sage, and lemon juice; mix with a spoon until well blended. Sprinkle with pepper to taste.

VARIATION: Try adding any medley of fresh herbs that you may have left over from other recipes or out in your garden, such as rosemary, basil, or cilantro. Start by adding 1 teaspoon at a time, taste, and then add more as desired.

SALSA

Whether the game is on or you're just lounging around with the family, a big bag of tortilla chips and a bowl of fresh salsa is always a welcome sight! In fact, the only thing better than seeing a fresh bowl of salsa is seeing two fresh bowls of salsa. Chips and salsa is just a classic combination; even sweet salsas have a crunchy companion in cinnamon tortilla chips. But salsa isn't just for chips!

Any of the salsas in this chapter would make a great topping for grilled or roasted meat, especially chicken or fish. Grilled chicken with Sweet Corn and Roasted Garlic Salsa (page 41), anyone? Maybe braised pork loin with Peach and Sweet Onion Salsa (page 38)? Perhaps it's a hot summer day and you're in the mood for a salad; top it with a big scoop of Cucumber Watermelon Salsa (page 45)! Salsas can also spice up your tacos and liven up a sandwich. I love having a bowl of salsa left over that I can use to fancy up lunch or dinner the next day. Salsa makes it simple to add an extra layer of flavor without having to do anything more than reach into the fridge!

Spicy Chipotle Salsa

Makes about 2 cups

1 (14.5-ounce) can fire-roasted diced tomatoes

2 chipotle peppers in adobo sauce, chopped

1 teaspoon adobo sauce

1 Roma tomato, diced

1 small onion, minced

2 cloves garlic, minced

$1/2$ jalapeño, seeded and minced

1 teaspoon salt

$1/2$ teaspoon black pepper

$1/4$ cup chopped fresh cilantro

Juice of 1 lime

Drain and discard about half the liquid from the can of tomatoes. Add the remaining tomatoes and their juice to a bowl with the chipotle peppers, adobo sauce, tomato, onion, garlic, jalapeño, salt, pepper, cilantro, and lime juice. Use a spoon to mix well.

....

CAUTION!

Hot chiles contain oils that will irritate the skin and leave you with a burning sensation. It is particularly painful if the oils get into your eyes or onto sensitive areas of skin. Anytime you are working with hot chiles, you should wear gloves and be sure to keep them away from your face!

Pico de Gallo

Makes about 2 cups

2 large ripe tomatoes, diced

1 small red onion, diced

1 jalapeño, seeded and minced

2 tablespoons minced fresh cilantro

1 tablespoon freshly squeezed lime juice

1 teaspoon salt

Fresh cilantro, for garnish

Combine all of the ingredients in a bowl and mix well with a spoon. Garnish with cilantro leaves.

VARIATIONS: Add a diced avocado and mix in gently. For a hotter salsa, use a Serrano pepper instead of a jalapeño.

Hearty Guacamole

Makes about 2 cups

2 ripe Hass avocados, cubed

$^1/_2$ red onion, minced

2 cloves garlic, minced

1 Roma tomato, diced

1 teaspoon salt

1 jalapeño, seeded and minced

$^1/_4$ cup chopped fresh cilantro

Juice of 1 lime

Combine all of the ingredients in a bowl. Using a spoon, gently mix everything together well, being careful not to smash the avocado too much.

VARIATIONS: For a touch of grilled flavor, rub each avocado half with a bit of oil and grill on high for 2 minutes to char. Get a sweet crunch by adding $^1/_2$ cup leftover sweet corn to the mix.

Salsa Verde

Makes about 2 cups

1 (7-ounce) can diced green
  chiles

1/2 yellow onion, diced

4 small tomatillos, hulled and quartered

1 jalapeño, seeded

1 teaspoon freshly squeezed lime juice

1 teaspoon salt

1/4 cup fresh cilantro

Combine all of the ingredients in a food processor or blender and blend until smooth.

VARIATION: For a smoky flavor, grill the onion, tomatillos, and jalapeño until charred and blistered.

Pineapple and Cilantro Salsa

Makes about 3 cups

2 cups diced fresh pineapple
¹/₄ cup chopped fresh cilantro
¹/₄ cup diced red onion
1 jalapeño, seeded and minced

Zest and juice of 1 lime
¹/₄ teaspoon salt
1 tablespoon brown sugar

Combine all of the ingredients in a bowl and mix well with a spoon. Refrigerate for at least 1 hour before serving.

VARIATION: For Piña Colada Salsa, mix in ¹/₄ cup shredded coconut.

Roasted Red Pepper and Rosemary Salsa

Makes about 3 cups

1 (16-ounce) jar roasted red peppers, drained and diced

1 tablespoon olive oil

3 tablespoons chopped fresh basil

1 Roma tomato, diced

1 tablespoon balsamic vinegar

2 cloves garlic, minced

$1/2$ teaspoon salt

$1/2$ teaspoon finely chopped fresh rosemary

Rosemary leaves, for garnish

Combine all of the ingredients in a bowl and mix well with a spoon. Garnish with whole rosemary leaves.

VARIATION: Add a bit of heat and a cheesy undertone with 1 teaspoon red pepper flakes and 2 tablespoons grated Parmesan cheese.

Peach and Sweet Onion Salsa

Makes about 3 cups

3 medium peaches, peeled and diced

2 Roma tomatoes, diced

1 medium sweet onion,* minced

1 teaspoon freshly squeezed lemon juice

1 teaspoon honey

1 teaspoon brown sugar

1 teaspoon salt

$1/_4$ cup chopped fresh chives, for garnish

Combine all of the ingredients in a bowl and mix well with a spoon. The salsa can be served immediately, but it is best to refrigerate and allow the flavors to meld for 2 to 3 hours, or overnight. Do not make this salsa too far ahead, or the peaches will start to turn on you. Garnish with fresh chives before serving.

There are many sweet onions that would work well for this recipe. Walla Walla, Vidalia, Maui, or cipollini would be just right. My all-time favorite is cipollini, but its shape can be a challenge to work with.

Sweet Corn and Roasted Garlic Salsa

Makes 3 cups

1 head garlic

1 teaspoon vegetable oil

1 (15.25-ounce) can sweet corn, drained

1 green bell pepper, seeded and diced

1 jalapeño, seeded and minced

1 small red onion, diced

2 tablespoons chopped fresh cilantro

1 tablespoon freshly squeezed lime juice

1 tablespoon honey

1 teaspoon apple cider vinegar

1 teaspoon salt

Preheat the oven to 350°F. Slice the top off of the head of garlic and discard. Drizzle garlic with the oil. Place garlic on a baking sheet and bake for 25 minutes, or until the skin and exposed garlic are both lightly browned. Set aside and allow to cool.

In a bowl, combine the corn, bell pepper, jalapeño, onion, cilantro, lime juice, honey, vinegar, and salt. Use a spoon to mix well. When the garlic is cool enough to handle, squeeze each clove from the uncut end of the head, and the cloves will slide out of the husk. Add the roasted garlic to the salsa and mix well.

VARIATION: For some extra sweetness, substitute roasted red pepper for the bell pepper.

Grape and Feta Salsa

Makes about 3 cups

2 oranges, peeled

1 cup red grapes, halved

1 small red onion, minced

$^1/_2$ cup crumbled feta cheese

2 tablespoons minced fresh basil

$^1/_4$ teaspoon black pepper

2 tablespoons olive oil

1 teaspoon balsamic vinegar

To segment your oranges, use a paring knife to slice a small piece off of the top and bottom of each orange to give you a stable cutting surface. Starting from the top of the orange, cut downward to peel away all of the rind and pith. Work your way around until the orange is completely peeled. Use a bowl to catch the juice and segments as you cut the orange. Take the orange in one hand, and using a paring knife, cut in along the membrane to the center of the orange. Cut each segment, leaving the membrane behind until all of the segments have been removed. Squeeze the remaining membrane of all its juice and discard.

In the bowl with the oranges, add the grapes, onion, feta, basil, pepper, olive oil, and vinegar. Use a spoon to mix well; refrigerate for 1 hour before serving.

VARIATION: For a sweeter flavor to complement the feta, top the salsa with golden raisins before serving.

Cucumber Watermelon Salsa

Makes about 3 cups

2 tablespoons honey

Juice of 1 lime

2 cups chopped seedless watermelon

$1/2$ cup peeled, seeded, and diced
  cucumber

$1/4$ cup diced red onion

$1/4$ cup diced red bell pepper

1 jalapeño, seeded and minced

2 tablespoons chopped fresh cilantro

1 tablespoon minced fresh mint

1 tablespoon minced fresh basil

In a bowl, mix the honey and the lime juice. Add the watermelon, cucumber, onion, bell pepper, jalapeño, cilantro, mint, and basil. Mix everything together with a spoon, being careful not to break up the watermelon too much.

VARIATION: For Melon Medley Salsa, add $1/2$ cup diced cantaloupe and $1/2$ cup diced honeydew. For a play on a classic hors d'oeuvre, garnish the bowl of salsa with $1/2$ cup thinly sliced prosciutto.

Bacon, Tomato, and Avocado Salsa

Makes about 4 cups

4 tablespoons chopped crispy-cooked
bacon pieces (about 6 strips)

2 Haas avocados, diced

2 large Roma tomatoes, diced

1 small red onion, minced

2 tablespoons chopped fresh cilantro

Juice of 1 lime

$1/2$ teaspoon salt

Black pepper

Combine the bacon, avocados, tomatoes, onion, cilantro, lime juice, and salt in a bowl; mix well with a spoon. Sprinkle with pepper to taste.

VARIATION: Add $1/4$ cup crumbled blue cheese and top with green onions.

Caprese Salsa

2 Roma tomatoes, diced

1/2 cup chopped fresh basil

4 ounces fresh mozzarella, diced

2 tablespoons olive oil, divided

1 teaspoon balsamic vinegar

Salt and black pepper

Place the tomatoes, basil, mozzarella, and 1 tablespoon of the olive oil in a bowl; mix well with a spoon. Transfer to a serving bowl and drizzle with balsamic vinegar and the remaining olive oil just before serving. Sprinkle with salt and pepper to taste.

VARIATION: For more Italian flavor and a heartier salsa, top with thinly sliced prosciutto or pepperoni.

Minty Cucumber Salsa

4 cucumbers, peeled, seeded, and diced

1 small red onion, diced

1/4 cup chopped fresh cilantro

1 jalapeño, seeded and minced

2 tablespoons chopped fresh mint

Juice of 2 limes

1/2 teaspoon salt

1 tablespoon olive oil

Combine all of the ingredients in a bowl and mix well with a spoon. Refrigerate for 1 hour before serving.

VARIATION: To make Lemon Cucumber Salsa, add the segments of 1 lemon and 1 tablespoon honey.

Black Bean and Avocado Salsa

2 Haas avocados, diced

1 (15-ounce) can black beans, drained and rinsed

1 cup frozen sweet corn kernels, thawed and drained

1 Roma tomato, diced

1 small red onion, diced

1/4 cup chopped fresh cilantro

2 tablespoons olive oil

Juice of 1 lime

1 clove garlic, minced

1 tablespoon apple cider vinegar

1 teaspoon salt

Combine all ingredients in a bowl and mix well with a spoon. Refrigerate for 1 hour before serving.

VARIATION: For White Bean and Avocado Salsa, substitute navy beans for the black beans.

PESTO

Pesto is usually a blend of garlic, basil, olive oil, pine nuts, and Parmesan cheese, but that's just one way to do it. By using a variety of herbs, nuts, and other ingredients, you can create a pesto that works well as a dip, a sandwich spread, or a sauce for cooked pasta.

One unique thing about pesto is its ability to handle heat. Give your classic chicken noodle soup an upgrade by tossing your chicken in some Rosemary Lemon Pesto (page 81). Try finishing your next batch of stir-fry with a big scoop of Cilantro Peanut Pesto (page 55) just before it comes out of the wok.

Pesto is versatile enough to top or stir into just about anything, including other dips! Top a batch of White Bean Hummus (page 85) or Sweet Corn and Roasted Garlic Salsa (page 41) with a hearty spoonful of Spinach Almond Pesto (page 62) for a delightfully different medley of flavors. Stirring in a tablespoon of Sun-Dried Tomato Pesto (page 65) could even liven up those bottles of Italian vinaigrette, ranch, or mayo that have been sitting in your fridge for a while.

Cilantro Peanut Pesto

Makes about 2 cups

½ cup unsalted roasted peanuts

2 cloves garlic

1 jalapeño, seeded

1 tablespoon grated fresh ginger

Zest and juice of 1 lime

1 cup fresh cilantro

¼ cup olive oil, divided

1 tablespoon honey

1 teaspoon fish sauce

In a blender or food processor, pulse the peanuts, garlic, and jalapeño until roughly chopped. Add the ginger, lime zest and juice, cilantro, and 4 tablespoons of the olive oil; pulse until no whole leaves of cilantro remain. Add the honey and fish sauce, and drizzle the remaining olive oil into the mixture while blending.

VARIATION: For a creamy pesto with a hint of sweetness, substitute coconut milk for the olive oil and pulse in ¼ cup grated coconut at the end.

Artichoke Citrus Pesto

Makes about 2 cups

1 (8-ounce) bag frozen artichoke
    hearts, thawed and drained

2 cloves garlic

1/2 cup fresh parsley

1/2 cup fresh spinach

1/2 cup fresh basil leaves

Zest and juice of 1 lemon

Zest and juice of 1 orange

Zest and juice of 1 lime

1/2 teaspoon salt

1/2 teaspoon black pepper

1/2 cup olive oil, divided

In a blender or food processor, pulse the artichoke hearts, garlic, parsley, spinach, and basil until roughly chopped. Add the lemon zest and juice, orange zest and juice, lime zest and juice, salt, pepper, and 1/4 cup of the olive oil; pulse until mixed. Drizzle the remaining olive oil into the mixture while blending.

VARIATION: This recipe contains no nuts or cheese, making it versatile for anyone with allergies to either. To make it a more traditional pesto, simply add 1/4 cup pine nuts in the first step of the recipe, and pulse in 1/4 cup grated Parmesan cheese at the end.

Olive and Watercress Pesto

Makes about 2 cups

¹/₂ cup shelled walnuts

1 clove garlic

¹/₄ cup olive oil, divided

¹/₂ cup fresh watercress

¹/₂ cup fresh spinach

¹/₂ cup kalamata olives, rinsed and pitted

¹/₂ cup grated Parmesan cheese

In a blender or food processor, pulse the walnuts and garlic until roughly chopped. Add 4 tablespoons of the olive oil, watercress, and spinach; pulse until no whole leaves remain. Drizzle the remaining olive oil into the mixture while blending. Add the olives and pulse to roughly chop. Add the Parmesan and pulse to mix.

VARIATION: If you want to try this recipe but are not fond of the pronounced flavor of kalamata olives, try substituting the kalamatas with Castelvetrano olives. They are a sweeter, milder type of olive that works well in this pesto.

Pistachio and Lemon Pesto

Makes about 2 cups

1 cup unsalted roasted pistachios	1 teaspoon salt
1 clove garlic	$1/2$ cup olive oil, divided
Zest and juice of 2 lemons	1 tablespoon chopped fresh mint
$1/2$ cup fresh basil leaves	$1/2$ cup grated pecorino cheese

In a blender or food processor, pulse the pistachios and garlic until roughly chopped. Add the lemon zest and juice, basil, salt, and $1/4$ cup of the olive oil; pulse until no whole leaves remain. Drizzle the remaining olive oil into the mixture while blending. Add the mint and pecorino cheese and pulse to mix.

VARIATION: Substituting half of the pecorino cheese for soft goat cheese will lend a creamy texture and subtle goat cheese flavor.

Spinach Almond Pesto

Makes about 2 cups

1 cup toasted slivered almonds

2 cloves garlic

2 cups fresh spinach

Zest and juice of 1 lemon

$^1/_2$ cup olive oil, divided

1 teaspoon salt

$^1/_2$ cup soft goat cheese

In a blender or food processor, pulse the almonds and garlic until roughly chopped. Add the spinach, lemon zest and juice, and $^1/_4$ cup of the olive oil; pulse until no whole leaves remain. Drizzle the remaining olive oil into the mixture while blending. Add the salt and goat cheese and pulse to mix.

VARIATION: If you aren't a fan of goat cheese, substitute grated pecorino cheese.

Sun-Dried Tomato Pesto

Makes about 2 cups

½ cup dry-packed sun-dried tomatoes

4 cloves garlic

¼ cup pine nuts

2 tablespoons tomato paste

½ cup olive oil, divided

1 cup fresh basil leaves

¼ cup balsamic vinegar

1 teaspoon salt

½ cup grated Parmesan cheese

In a blender or food processor, pulse the tomatoes, garlic, pine nuts, and tomato paste until roughly chopped. Add ¼ cup of the olive oil, basil, balsamic vinegar, and salt. Drizzle the remaining olive oil into the mixture while blending. Add the Parmesan and pulse to mix.

VARIATION: For a smoky, slightly sweet pesto, substitute ¼ cup of the sun-dried tomatoes for roasted red peppers.

Honey Pecan Pesto

Makes about 2 cups

1/2 cup pecan pieces

1 small shallot

1/4 cup olive oil, divided

1 cup fresh basil leaves

1/2 cup fresh parsley

2 tablespoons honey

1 tablespoon champagne vinegar

1 teaspoon salt

1/2 teaspoon Dijon mustard

In a blender or food processor, pulse the pecans and shallot until roughly chopped. Add 4 tablespoons of the olive oil, basil, and parsley; pulse until no whole leaves remain. Add the honey, vinegar, salt, and mustard. Drizzle the remaining olive oil into the mixture while blending.

VARIATION: For more texture and a fruity flavor, stir in 1/2 cup minced green apple or pear to the finished pesto.

No-Nut Basil Pesto

Makes about 1 cup

3 cloves garlic

1/2 cup olive oil

2 cups fresh basil leaves

Zest and juice of 1 lemon

1 teaspoon salt

1/2 cup grated Parmesan cheese

In a blender or food processor, pulse garlic with 1/4 cup of oil until roughly chopped. Add basil and pulse until no whole leaves remain. Add zest and juice and salt; drizzle remaining oil into the mixture while blending. Add Parmesan cheese and pulse to mix.

Apple Pepita Pesto

Makes about 2 cups

2 cups pepitas (hulled pumpkin seeds)

3 cloves garlic

1/2 cup fresh spinach

1/4 cup fresh cilantro

1/2 teaspoon salt

1/4 cup olive oil, divided

Zest and juice of 1 lemon

1/2 cup diced green apple

In a blender or food processor, pulse pepitas and garlic until roughly chopped. Add spinach, cilantro, salt, and 4 tablespoons of oil; pulse until no whole spinach leaves remain. Add zest and juice, and drizzle remaining oil into the mixture while blending. Add apple and pulse to mix.

Hot Chile Pepper Pesto

Makes about 2 cups

¼ cup pine nuts

2 cloves garlic

¼ cup olive oil, divided

1 cup fresh basil leaves

½ cup pickled hot chile peppers, such as jalapeños

½ cup roasted red peppers

½ cup grated Parmesan cheese

In a blender or food processor, pulse the pine nuts and garlic until roughly chopped. Add 4 tablespoons of the olive oil and the basil; pulse until no whole leaves remain. Drizzle the remaining olive oil into the mixture while blending. Add the chile peppers, red peppers, and Parmesan; pulse to mix.

VARIATIONS: The pickled peppers add some acidity and salt to this pesto. For a fresher flavor, you can substitute ½ cup fresh chile peppers, seeded, for the pickled chile peppers. For a mellower flavor, substitute ¼ cup of the hot peppers with sweet peppers, such as piquillos.

Arugula and Parsley Pesto

Makes about 2 cups

1/4 cup slivered almonds

1/4 cup shelled walnuts

1 clove garlic

2 cups fresh arugula

1/2 cup fresh parsley

1/2 cup olive oil, divided

1 teaspoon salt

1 teaspoon freshly squeezed lemon juice

1/2 cup grated Parmesan cheese

In a blender or food processor, pulse the almonds, walnuts, and garlic until roughly chopped. Add the arugula, parsley, and 1/4 cup of the olive oil; pulse until no whole arugula leaves remain. Add the salt and lemon juice; drizzle the remaining olive oil into the mixture while blending. Add the Parmesan and pulse to mix.

VARIATION: If you get a particularly strong batch of arugula, or just want to mellow out the flavor, substitute 1 cup of the arugula with fresh spinach.

Basil and Walnut Pesto

Makes about 2 cups

$^1/_2$ cup shelled walnuts

4 cloves garlic

2 cups fresh basil leaves

$^1/_2$ teaspoon salt

$^1/_2$ cup olive oil, divided

$^1/_4$ cup grated Parmesan cheese

In a blender or food processor, pulse the walnuts and garlic together until roughly chopped. Add the basil, salt, and $^1/_4$ cup of the olive oil; pulse until no whole basil leaves remain. Drizzle the remaining olive oil into the mixture while blending. Add the Parmesan and pulse until everything is evenly mixed.

VARIATION: For a brighter taste, add the zest and juice of 1 large grapefruit.

Avocado Mint Pesto

$^1/_4$ cup pine nuts

2 cloves garlic

2 Haas avocados, diced

2 teaspoons salt

1 teaspoon freshly squeezed lemon juice

$^1/_4$ cup olive oil

2 tablespoons minced fresh mint

In a blender or food processor, pulse the pine nuts and garlic until roughly chopped. Add the avocado, salt, and lemon juice; blend until smooth. Drizzle in the olive oil while blending. Add the mint and pulse to mix.

VARIATION: This recipe yields a very smooth pesto. If you want to add a bit of creaminess, reduce the salt to 1 teaspoon and add $^1/_4$ cup of soft goat cheese with the mint.

Jalapeño, Spinach, and Cilantro Pesto

Makes about 2 cups

¹/₄ cup pine nuts

2 cloves garlic

2 jalapeños, seeded

2 cups fresh spinach

¹/₂ cup fresh cilantro

¹/₂ cup olive oil, divided

Zest and juice of 1 lemon

1 teaspoon salt

¹/₂ cup grated pecorino cheese

In a blender or food processor, pulse the pine nuts, garlic, and the jalapeños until roughly chopped. Add the spinach, cilantro, and ¹/₄ cup of the olive oil; pulse until no whole spinach leaves remain. Add the lemon zest and juice and salt; drizzle the remaining olive oil into the mixture while blending. Add the pecorino cheese and pulse to mix.

VARIATION: The seeded jalapeños should offer a medium amount of heat. If you want more heat, substitute the jalapeños with Serrano peppers.

Kale Cashew Pesto

Makes about 2 cups

$^1/_2$ **cup cashews**	**2 cups fresh baby kale**
2 cloves garlic	$^1/_2$ **cup olive oil, divided**
1 teaspoon salt	$^1/_2$ **cup grated Romano cheese**
1 teaspoon freshly squeezed lemon juice	

In a blender or food processor, pulse the cashews and garlic until roughly chopped. Add the salt, lemon juice, kale, and $^1/_4$ cup of the olive oil; pulse until no whole leaves remain. Drizzle the remaining olive oil into the mixture while blending. Add the Romano cheese and pulse to mix.

VARIATION: If you want a more intense kale flavor, substitute another type of kale, such as curly leaf or red Russian, for the baby kale. With mature kale, be sure to remove the stems. If the finished pesto turns out too bitter, add 1 tablespoon of honey at a time until the flavor is adjusted to your liking.

Rosemary Lemon Pesto

Makes about 2 cups

$^1/_2$ cup almonds

2 cloves garlic

$^1/_2$ cup fresh basil leaves

$^1/_2$ cup fresh spinach

$^1/_4$ cup fresh rosemary leaves

Zest and juice of 2 lemons

1 teaspoon salt

$^1/_2$ cup olive oil, divided

$^1/_4$ cup grated Parmesan cheese

In a blender or food processor, pulse the almonds and garlic until roughly chopped. Add the basil, spinach, rosemary, lemon zest and juice, salt, and $^1/_4$ cup of the olive oil; pulse until no whole spinach leaves remain. Drizzle in the remaining olive oil while blending. Add the Parmesan and pulse to mix.

VARIATION: If there is too much rosemary for your taste, substitute 4 tablespoons of the rosemary with fresh parsley.

HUMMUS

These hummus recipes can be made with canned beans or boiled dry beans. Hummus is traditionally made with chickpeas (also called garbanzo beans), but navy beans and black beans make delicious variations. (Edamame are another good stand-in for chickpeas; you can simply buy the frozen pods, defrost them, and you are good to go.) If you decide to use dry beans, it's best to soak them overnight in cold water, then boil them in unsalted water until tender. The amount of time it takes to cook dried beans varies depending on the type of bean you're cooking, the size of the beans, how old the beans are, and whether they've been soaked or not. Every batch will be different, but it shouldn't take more than two hours of simmering to get nice, soft beans that will still hold their shape.

Hummus is bold enough to be scooped and eaten on pita bread or crackers, and it will liven up the simplest of fresh vegetables. It's also a surprisingly fantastic addition to sandwiches and even grilled meats or vegetables. Try it spread on a tuna salad sandwich instead of mayo, or reach for some Kale and Almond Hummus (page 96) for your baked chicken and rice. If you end up with some leftover hummus, you can store it in the refrigerator for up to 7 days and in the freezer for several months.

Basic Hummus

Makes about 3 cups

2 (15-ounce) cans chickpeas, drained and rinsed

4 cloves garlic

1/2 cup water

1/4 cup tahini

2 tablespoons olive oil

3 tablespoons freshly squeezed lemon juice

1 tablespoon sesame oil

1 teaspoon salt

1/2 teaspoon ground cumin

Combine all of the ingredients in a food processor or blender and blend until smooth.

TAHINI

Tahini is a paste made from sesame seeds. It can be found in some supermarkets and most specialty food stores. It's rather simple to make your own though. Any sesame seeds, hulled, unhulled (natural), sprouted, raw, or toasted, will work to make tahini, but hulled seeds result in a smoother and less bitter paste. To make 1/2 cup of tahini, start with 1 cup of hulled sesame seeds. Place the seeds in a food processor and blend them until they resemble damp sand. Add 3 tablespoons of canola oil or light olive oil and continue to blend until a smooth paste forms. You may need to scrape the bowl of the food processor to make sure everything is well blended. Store the tahini in a sealed container in the fridge for up to 1 week. If the oil separates, just mix it well before using.

Olive and Rosemary Hummus

Makes about 2 cups

1 (15-ounce) can chickpeas

2 cloves garlic

1/2 cup kalamata olives, rinsed and pitted

2 tablespoons tahini (page 83)

1/2 teaspoon salt

1/4 teaspoon ground cumin

1/4 cup water

2 tablespoons chopped fresh rosemary

2 tablespoons olive oil

1 tablespoon sesame oil

Combine all of the ingredients in a food processor or blender and blend until smooth.

White Bean Hummus

Makes about 3 cups

2 (15-ounce) cans navy beans, drained and rinsed

2 cloves garlic

2 tablespoons freshly squeezed lemon juice

1/4 teaspoon ground cumin

2 tablespoons tahini (page 83)

1/2 teaspoon salt

1/4 cup olive oil

Combine all of the ingredients in a food processor or blender and blend until smooth.

Black Bean Chipotle Hummus

Makes about 2 cups

1 (15-ounce) can black beans, drained and rinsed

1 clove garlic

1/2 teaspoon ground cumin

2 tablespoons olive oil

1 tablespoon tahini (page 83)

2 chipotle peppers in adobo sauce

1 tablespoon adobo sauce

2 tablespoons chopped fresh cilantro

1/2 teaspoon salt

Fresh cilantro, for garnish

Combine all of the ingredients in a food processor or blender and blend until smooth. Transfer the hummus to a serving dish and garnish with cilantro leaves.

Roasted Beet Hummus

Makes about 2 cups

3 medium-size red beets, diced, or 1 can diced beets, drained

1 tablespoon canola oil

1 (15-ounce) can chickpeas, drained

2 cloves garlic

2 tablespoons tahini (page 83)

1 tablespoon sesame oil

2 tablespoons olive oil

$1/2$ teaspoon ground cumin

1 teaspoon salt

2 tablespoons freshly squeezed lemon juice

Preheat the oven to 400°F. In a large bowl, toss the diced beets with the canola oil. Transfer the beets to a baking sheet and bake for 15 minutes, or until the beets have softened in the center. Set aside to cool.

Combine the chickpeas, garlic, tahini, sesame oil, olive oil, cumin, salt, and lemon juice in a blender or food processor; blend until smooth. Add the roasted beets and continue to blend until smooth.

Roasted Red Pepper and Herb Hummus

Makes about 2 cups

1 (15-ounce) can chickpeas, drained

2 cloves garlic

2 tablespoons tahini (page 83)

2 tablespoons freshly squeezed lemon juice

1 teaspoon salt

3 tablespoons olive oil, divided

$^3/_4$ cup diced roasted red peppers, divided

$^1/_4$ cup toasted pine nuts

1 teaspoon ground marjoram

1 tablespoon chopped fresh parsley

1 tablespoon chopped fresh rosemary

Combine the chickpeas, garlic, tahini, lemon juice, salt, 2 tablespoons of the olive oil, and half of the red peppers in a food processor or blender; blend until smooth. Transfer the hummus to a serving dish and set aside.

In a small bowl, mix the remaining red peppers, remaining olive oil, pine nuts, marjoram, parsley, and rosemary. Sprinkle the pine nut and herb mixture on the hummus and serve.

Cucumber Yogurt Hummus

Makes about 3 cups

1/4 cup cucumber pulp

1 (15-ounce) can chickpeas, drained

1 clove garlic

1 teaspoon salt

2 tablespoons freshly squeezed lemon juice

2/3 cup Greek yogurt

2 tablespoons tahini (page 83)

Combine all of the ingredients in a food processor or blender and blend until smooth.

CUCUMBER PULP

To make cucumber pulp, use medium-size ripe cucumbers. Peel them, cut them in half lengthwise, and scrape the seeds out with a spoon and discard. Cut the cucumbers into 1-inch-long pieces, then blend in a food processor or blender until smooth. Strain the mixture through a fine mesh sieve, pressing lightly with the back of a spoon to remove the liquid. Using a layer of cheesecloth in the sieve helps to reduce the amount of pulp that makes its way through the strainer. Once the mixture is thick and holds a shape, it is ready to use. Four medium cucumbers usually yield about 1/4 cup of pulp.

Pumpkin Pepita Hummus

Makes about 3 cups

$^1/_2$ cup toasted pepitas (hulled
  pumpkin seeds), divided

1 tablespoon olive oil

1 tablespoon sesame oil

1 (15-ounce) can pumpkin

1 (15-ounce) can chickpeas, drained

2 tablespoons tahini (page 83)

1 clove garlic

2 tablespoons freshly squeezed lemon
  juice

1 teaspoon ground cumin

$^1/_2$ teaspoon salt

Combine $^1/_4$ cup of the pepitas, olive oil, and sesame oil in a food processor or blender; blend until smooth. Add the pumpkin, chickpeas, tahini, garlic, lemon juice, cumin, and salt; blend well. Transfer the hummus to a serving dish and garnish with the remaining pepitas.

Baba Ghanoush Hummus

Makes about 3 cups

1 large eggplant

¹/₄ cup tahini (page 83)

1 tablespoon olive oil

1 tablespoon sesame oil

1 (15-ounce) can chickpeas, drained

4 cloves garlic

3 tablespoons freshly squeezed lemon juice

1 teaspoon salt

¹/₂ teaspoon ground cumin

Preheat the oven to 450°F. Poke the eggplant all over with a fork and place on a baking sheet. Bake for about 20 minutes, until you can feel the flesh starting to soften under the skin. Cool eggplant completely, cut in half lengthwise, drain off any excess liquid, and scrape out the flesh.

Place the eggplant flesh in a blender or food processor; blend with the tahini, olive oil, and sesame oil until smooth. Add the chickpeas, garlic, lemon juice, salt, and cumin; blend until smooth.

Edamame and Soy Hummus

Makes about 3 cups

2 cups frozen shelled edamame, thawed

2 cloves garlic

$^1/_4$ cup tahini (page 83)

2 tablespoons soy sauce

$^1/_4$ cup water

2 tablespoons freshly squeezed lemon juice

3 tablespoons olive oil

$^1/_2$ teaspoon ground cumin

1 tablespoon sesame oil

Sesame seeds, for garnish

Combine all of the ingredients in a food processor or blender and blend until smooth. Transfer the hummus to a serving dish and garnish with sesame seeds.

Kale and Almond Hummus

Makes about 3 cups

3 cups stemmed kale

$1/2$ cup sliced almonds, divided

1 (15-ounce) can chickpeas, drained

$1/4$ cup olive oil

2 tablespoons freshly squeezed lemon
  juice

2 cloves garlic

$1/4$ cup tahini (page 83)

$1/2$ teaspoon salt

2 tablespoons sesame oil

In a blender of food processor, pulse the kale and $1/4$ cup of the almonds until roughly chopped. Add the chickpeas, olive oil, lemon juice, garlic, tahini, salt, and sesame oil; blend until smooth. Transfer the hummus to a serving dish and garnish with the remaining almonds.

Coconut Curry Hummus

Makes about 3 cups

2 (15-ounce) cans chickpeas, drained

$1/2$ cup coconut milk

1 tablespoon red curry paste, plus
   more as needed

1 clove garlic

$1/2$ teaspoon salt

1 tablespoon tahini (page 83)

Zest and juice of 1 lime

1 tablespoon sesame oil

Combine all of the ingredients in a food processor or blender and blend until smooth. Curry paste can vary greatly in saltiness and spiciness, so taste the hummus and add more if needed.

Avocado Feta Hummus

Makes about 3 cups

1 (15-ounce) can navy beans, drained and rinsed

1 Haas avocado, diced

2 tablespoons freshly squeezed lemon juice

1 clove garlic

1 teaspoon salt

1 tablespoon tahini (page 83)

2 tablespoons olive oil

1/2 cup fresh spinach

1/4 cup feta crumbles, for garnish

Combine all of the ingredients in a food processor or blender; blend until smooth. Transfer the hummus to a serving dish and garnish with the feta.

Lemon, Almond, and Poppy Hummus

Makes about 3 cups

1 cup blanched slivered almonds

2 tablespoons olive oil

1 tablespoon sesame oil

2 tablespoons tahini (page 83)

1 (15-ounce) can chickpeas, drained

2 cloves garlic

¹/₂ cup freshly squeezed lemon juice

3 tablespoons honey

Sliced almonds, for garnish

1 ¹/₂ tablespoons poppy seeds, for garnish

Combine the slivered almonds, olive oil, sesame oil, and tahini in a food processor or blender; blend until smooth. Add the chickpeas, garlic, lemon juice, and honey; blend until smooth. Transfer the hummus to a serving dish and garnish with sliced almonds and poppy seeds.

SOUR CREAM

One of my favorite things to do in the summertime is to head to the farmer's market and pick up some fresh produce. Fresh radishes, purple carrots, rainbows of tomatoes, and piles of freshly picked green beans head home with me and often end up being enjoyed in a dip made with sour cream.

Each of the recipes in this section uses sour cream as the base, and it doesn't matter if it's fat free, reduced fat, or just plain sour cream. While all of these dips are delicious with a bag of potato chips, a box of your favorite crackers, or a stack of raw vegetable sticks, many are also delicious as a sauce for meats and sandwiches. Horseradish Chive Dip (page 103) is fantastic served alongside a thick grilled rib-eye steak. A chicken salad sandwich with a bit of Cucumber Dill Dip (page 116) makes a great addition to a springtime lunch, and even a microwave burrito will sound good smothered with a big scoop of Creamy Avocado Dip (page 109)!

Horseradish Chive Dip

Makes about 2 cups

1 cup sour cream

1/2 cup mayonnaise

1/4 cup minced chives

1/2 teaspoon salt

1/2 teaspoon black pepper

1 tablespoon freshly squeezed lemon juice

1 teaspoon balsamic vinegar

1 tablespoon grated horseradish, plus more as needed

In a large bowl, combine all of the ingredients except the horseradish; mix with a whisk. Horseradish can vary greatly in heat and intensity so start with 1 tablespoon, mix it into the dip, and then taste. Continue adding 1 teaspoon at a time until the flavor is just right.

VARIATION: Garnish with 1 tablespoon of fresh thyme and a drizzle of olive oil to add an extra layer of flavor.

Roasted Chile and Lime Dip

Makes about 2 cups

1 cup sour cream

$^1/_2$ cup Mexican crema

2 (7-ounce) cans diced green chiles

1 teaspoon chili powder

Zest and juice of 2 limes

2 tablespoons chopped fresh cilantro

1 teaspoon salt

1 jalapeño, seeded and minced

In a large bowl, combine all of the ingredients and mix with a whisk. Do not overwhip or the Mexican crema may start to curdle.

VARIATION: For Chile Relleno Dip, add $^1/_2$ cup grated smoked Gouda.

MEXICAN CREMA

Mexican crema is available at most supermarkets, but if you are having a hard time finding it, you can make your own. Mix 1 cup sour cream with 1 cup heavy cream and place in a covered container. Leave mixture at room temperature for 4 hours, then refrigerate for at least 2 hours, or overnight. Because there is a high butterfat content, the crema can be whipped to make it lighter and fluffier, much like a savory whipped cream. Overwhipping will result in the butterfat separating, causing the mixture to curdle, so make sure to not whip it past stiff peaks.

Wasabi Ginger Dip

Makes about 3 cups

2 tablespoons wasabi paste,* plus
   more as needed

2 tablespoons grated fresh ginger

Zest and juice of 1 lemon

2 cups sour cream

$1/4$ cup rice wine vinegar

$1/4$ cup minced green onion

1 jalapeño, seeded and minced

Sesame seeds, for garnish

In a large bowl, combine all of the ingredients and mix well with a whisk. The heat and intensity of wasabi can vary, so start with 2 tablespoons and increase by 1 teaspoon at a time if a more intense wasabi flavor is desired. Transfer to a serving dish and sprinkle with the sesame seeds.

Wasabi paste may be hard to find, but wasabi powder will work just as well. If using wasabi powder, follow the package instructions to hydrate it into a paste.

Shrimp Dip

Makes about 2 cups

1 cup sour cream

$^1/_4$ cup minced green onions

$^1/_4$ cup minced celery

$^1/_2$ pound cooked shrimp, peeled and diced

1 teaspoon Old Bay seasoning

1 tablespoon freshly squeezed lemon juice

1 teaspoon fresh dill

$^1/_2$ teaspoon celery salt

In a large bowl, combine all of the ingredients and mix well with a large spoon.

Creamy Avocado Dip

Makes about 3 cups

1 cup sour cream

2 Haas avocados, diced

1/4 cup chopped green onion

1 teaspoon freshly squeezed lemon juice

1 teaspoon freshly squeezed lime juice

1 teaspoon ground cumin

2 teaspoons chili powder

1/2 teaspoon salt

1/4 cup chopped fresh cilantro

1/2 cup Mexican crema (page 104), whipped to soft peaks

In a blender or food processor, blend the avocado and sour cream until smooth. Transfer to a mixing bowl. Add the green onion, lemon juice, lime juice, cumin, chili powder, salt, and cilantro; mix well with a whisk. Fold in the Mexican crema with a spoon. Refrigerate for at least 2 hours before serving.

VARIATION: To make Spicy Avocado Lime Dip, add 1 jalapeño, seeded, 1 tablespoon freshly squeezed lime juice, and 1 teaspoon cayenne to the food processor.

Crab Louis Dip

Makes about 2 cups

1 cup sour cream

1 tablespoon cocktail sauce

1 teaspoon freshly squeezed lemon juice

2 tablespoons sweet relish

$1/4$ cup chopped black olives, plus
  more for garnish

$1/2$ cup lump crabmeat

1 avocado, diced

2 boiled eggs, diced, for garnish

Black pepper, for garnish

Fresh parsley, for garnish

In a large bowl, combine the sour cream, cocktail sauce, lemon juice, relish, and olives; mix well with a whisk. Fold in the crabmeat and avocado with a large spoon. Transfer to a serving dish and garnish with the eggs, olives, pepper, and fresh parsley.

VARIATION: For Seafood Louis Dip, substitute the crab for a medley of cooked shellfish.

Mushroom and Thyme Dip

2 tablespoons butter

1 pound cremini mushrooms, chopped

1 tablespoon fresh thyme

1 cup sour cream

1 teaspoon salt

1 teaspoon black pepper

1 teaspoon sherry (optional)

In a large pan, melt the butter over medium heat. Add the mushrooms and cook, stirring occasionally, until they have released all of their liquid, about 5 minutes. Continue to cook over medium heat until all of the liquid is evaporated, about 10 minutes. Remove the pan from the heat, stir in the thyme, and set aside to cool.

In a large bowl, combine the sour cream, salt, pepper, and sherry; mix with a whisk. Fold in the cooked mushrooms.

Buttermilk Herb Dip

Makes about 2 cups

1 cup sour cream

$^1/_4$ cup buttermilk

Zest and juice of 1 lemon

1 tablespoon minced fresh chives

1 tablespoon chopped fresh parsley

1 tablespoon fresh dill

1 tablespoon chopped fresh cilantro

2 cloves garlic, minced

2 small shallots, minced

$^1/_2$ teaspoon Dijon mustard

$^1/_2$ teaspoon salt

$^1/_2$ teaspoon black pepper

$^1/_2$ cup heavy cream, whipped to soft peaks

In a large bowl, combine all of the ingredients except the whipped cream; mix well with a spoon. Fold the whipped cream into the mixture. The cream will add a light and fluffy texture to this full-flavored dip.

VARIATION: To make Avocado Herb Dip, mix 2 Haas avocados, diced and mashed, into the sour cream before combining the rest of the ingredients.

Cucumber Dill Dip

Makes about 2 cups

1/4 cup cucumber pulp (page 91)

1 cup sour cream

1/2 cup Greek yogurt

3 cloves garlic, minced

Zest and juice of 2 lemons

1 tablespoon fresh dill

1 teaspoon minced fresh chives

1 teaspoon salt

1 tablespoon minced fresh mint, for garnish

In a large bowl, combine all of the ingredients and mix well with a whisk. Transfer to a serving bowl and garnish with the mint.

VARIATION: To make Chicken Souvlaki Dip, add 1/2 cup shredded cooked chicken, 1 teaspoon chopped fresh oregano, and 1 teaspoon lemon pepper.

Truffle Dip

Makes about 2 cups

1 cup sour cream

2 tablespoons minced fresh chives

2 tablespoons chopped fresh parsley

1 teaspoon salt

2 tablespoons black truffle oil

1/2 cup heavy cream, whipped to soft peaks

In a large bowl, combine the sour cream, chives, parsley, and salt; mix well with a whisk. In another bowl, fold the truffle oil into the whipped cream with a large spoon. Fold the truffle whipped cream into the sour cream mixture. If you want more of a truffle kick, garnish the dip with a light drizzle of truffle oil—a little bit will go a long way though!

VARIATION: For a lighter truffle flavor, substitute 2 tablespoons white truffle oil for the black truffle oil. White truffles have a mellow and slightly garlicky and peppery flavor.

Pad Thai Dip

Makes about 3 cups

3 tablespoons tamarind concentrate*
or Thai Kitchen pad thai sauce

3 tablespoons soy sauce

$^1/_4$ cup coconut milk

$^1/_4$ cup rice wine vinegar

2 tablespoons brown sugar

1 tablespoon honey

$^1/_4$ cup chopped fresh cilantro

Zest and juice of 1 lime

1 teaspoon peanut butter

1 cup sour cream

$^1/_4$ cup minced carrot

$^1/_4$ cup minced cauliflower

$^1/_4$ cup shelled frozen edamame, thawed

$^1/_4$ cup roasted peanuts, chopped, for garnish

Fresh cilantro, for garnish

In a large bowl, combine the tamarind concentrate, soy sauce, coconut milk, vinegar, brown sugar, honey, cilantro, lime zest and juice, and peanut butter; mix well with a whisk, making sure the honey and peanut butter are fully dissolved. Mix in the sour cream, carrot, cauliflower, and edamame with a large spoon. Transfer the dip to a serving bowl and garnish with the peanuts and cilantro.

VARIATION: Add $^1/_4$ cup of shredded cooked chicken or crumbled extra firm tofu to boost the protein in this hearty dip.

Tamarind concentrate can be found at Asian specialty markets or in the Asian section of some grocery stores.

Green Curry Coconut Dip

Makes about 3 cups

¹/₄ cup rice wine vinegar

¹/₄ cup coconut milk

¹/₄ cup chopped fresh cilantro

1 tablespoon green curry paste

Zest and juice of 1 lime

2 cups sour cream

¹/₂ cup minced green apple

Chopped green onion, for garnish

In a large bowl, combine the vinegar, coconut milk, cilantro, curry paste, and lime zest and juice; mix well with a whisk. Fold in the sour cream and apple with a large spoon. Transfer to a serving dish and garnish with the green onion.

BLT Dip

Makes about 2 cups

1 cup sour cream

$^1/_4$ cup mayonnaise

2 cloves garlic, minced

$^1/_2$ cup crispy-cooked bacon pieces

1 Roma tomato, seeded and diced

$^1/_2$ cup chopped fresh spinach

$^1/_2$ teaspoon salt

$^1/_2$ teaspoon black pepper

In a large bowl, combine all of the ingredients and mix well with a large spoon.

VARIATION: Add $^1/_2$ cup shredded Swiss cheese if you like your BLT with cheese.

Tangy Balsamic Dip

Makes about 2 cups

1 cup sour cream

1/4 cup balsamic vinegar

1/2 teaspoon salt

1/2 teaspoon granulated onion

1/2 teaspoon granulated garlic

1 tablespoon minced fresh parsley

1/2 cup Mexican crema (page 104), whipped to stiff peaks

Black pepper, for garnish

In a large bowl, combine the sour cream, vinegar, salt, onion, garlic, and parsley; mix with a whisk until well blended. Fold in the Mexican crema with a large spoon and refrigerate for 2 hours, or overnight. Top with pepper just before serving.

VARIATION: There are a lot of balsamic vinegars to choose from, and they all vary in acidity and flavor. Any balsamic vinegar will work in this recipe, but if you want to change things up, look for a flavored balsamic such as fig or wild blueberry.

Index

Metric Conversion Chart

VOLUME MEASUREMENTS		WEIGHT MEASUREMENTS		TEMPERATURE CONVERSION	
U.S.	METRIC	U.S.	METRIC	FAHRENHEIT	CELSIUS
1 teaspoon	5 ml	1/2 ounce	15 g	250	120
1 tablespoon	15 ml	1 ounce	30 g	300	150
1/4 cup	60 ml	3 ounces	90 g	325	160
1/3 cup	75 ml	4 ounces	115 g	350	180
1/2 cup	125 ml	8 ounces	225 g	375	190
2/3 cup	150 ml	12 ounces	350 g	400	200
3/4 cup	175 ml	1 pound	450 g	425	220
1 cup	250 ml	2 1/4 pounds	1 kg	450	230

To Breanna and Keisean,
my two favorite reasons to cook

20 19 18   5 4 3

Text © 2016 by James Bradford
Photographs © 2016 by Susan Hayward

Published by
Gibbs Smith
P.O. Box 667
Layton, Utah 84041

1.800.835.4993 orders
www.gibbs-smith.com

Designed by Katie Jennings
Prop styling and photography assistance by Annie Cheney

Gibbs Smith books are printed on paper produced from
sustainable PEFC-certified forest/controlled wood source.
Learn more at www.pefc.org.
Printed and bound in Hong Kong

Library of Congress Cataloging-in-Publication Data
Names: Bradford, James, author.
Title: Big dips : cheese, salsa, pesto, hummus / James
Bradford: photographs by Susan Barnson Hayward.
Description: First edition. | Layton, Utah : Gibbs Smith,
[2016] | Includes index.
Identifiers: LCCN 2016003197 | ISBN 9781423644538
Subjects: LCSH: Dips (Appetizers) | Salsas (Cooking) |
LCGFT: Cookbooks.
Classification: LCC TX819.A1 B67 2016 | DDC 641.81/2--dc23
LC record available at http://lccn.loc.gov/2016003197